The
BIBLE

The BIBLE

Dedicated to my nieces and nephews

—Sandra

To my husband and kids

—Shawnda

ISBN 13: 978-1-4621-4950-6

Published by CFI, an imprint of Cedar Fort, Inc.
2373 W. 700 S., Suite 100, Springville, UT 84663
Distributed by Cedar Fort, Inc., www.cedarfort.com

Library of Congress Control Number: 2025945549

Cover design and interior layout by Shawnda T. Craig

Edited by Kyle Lund

Printed in China

10 9 8 7 6 5 4 3 2 1

Printed on acid-free paper

The BIBLE

Written by **Sandra Meaders** Art by **Shawnda Craig**

THE
BIBLE

The Bible was written a long, long time ago.

The Bible contains many stories and lessons
to help people to learn to have faith in God.

THE BIBLE

The Bible was written in ancient languages that were translated into over 700 modern languages from Chinese, Spanish, Tongan, Portuguese, Swahili, French, and many, many more. That means friends from all over the world can read the Bible.

圣经
BIBLIA

The Bible is one of the most published books in the world with over five billion copies printed. That's a lot of books!

Many religions use the Bible and everyone who believes in it draws closer to God. The Bible has two parts: The Old Testament and the New Testament.

THE OLD TESTAMENT

The Old Testament explains that God created heaven, earth, animals, plants, light and darkness, night and day.

He created the world to help us learn and grow. The Old Testament also shares many stories about people who followed God.

Noah's Ark

God sent a flood to the earth to punish the wicked. God warned Noah, and he built an ark. Noah saved his family and many animals from the flood.

Joseph Helps Pharaoh

Pharaoh had dreams that scared him. Joseph was able to help Pharaoh understand that the dreams were a warning from God that there would be a great famine. Pharaoh helped his people to save enough food, so they would not be hungry.

Moses Parts the Red Sea

The ancient Israelites needed help. They were held captive and slaves to the Egyptians. Moses rescued them with God's help by parting the Red Sea.

Joshua Followed the Lord's Commandments

The Lord helped Joshua conquer Jericho. The Lord instructed Joshua to gather an army. They marched around the city for seven days as the priests blew their horns. On the seventh day, the city fell.

The Story of Ruth

Ruth took care of Naomi when her husband and son died. Ruth was a hard worker and kind. The Lord blessed her.

Hannah's Prayer

Hannah prayed for a child. Hannah promised the Lord that if she had a son, he would grow up to serve the Lord. The Lord blessed Hannah with a son named Samuel, who became a prophet.

THE NEW TESTAMENT

The New Testament shares stories surrounding Jesus's birth and life on earth. It also contains the stories of His apostles carrying forth Jesus's work after his death.

The Angel Visits Mary

Mary was visited by an angel. The angel told Mary that God blessed her, and she would be the mother of Jesus.

Jesus Is Born in Bethlehem

Mary and her husband, Joseph, travelled to Bethlehem to pay their taxes. The inns had no room. Mary gave birth to Jesus and laid him in a manger.

Young Jesus

Jesus travelled with His family to Jerusalem. Joseph and Mary lost Jesus and couldn't find Him for three days. They found him in the temple talking with teachers and answering their questions about God.

Jesus Is Baptized

Jesus came to John the Baptist to be baptized in the river Jordan. Jesus wanted to set an example for us to be baptized. Heavenly Father spoke and said, "This is my beloved Son, in whom I am well pleased."

Jesus Did Amazing Things!

Jesus healed the lepers,

helped the lame to walk,

and the blind to see.

Jesus turned water into wine,

fed many with very little food,

and raised the dead
to live again.

Jesus in Gethsemane

Jesus suffered for the pains and sins of the world in the Garden of Gethsemane.

Jesus's Resurrection

Jesus was crucified on a cross. After three days, Jesus was resurrected and lived again. He suffered for us, so that we may repent and live with Him again in heaven.

The Bible has inspired many artists, musicians and writers over the course of history.

Leonardo Da Vinci's
Last Supper

Michelangelo's **David**

composer of ***Messiah***,
George Frideric Handel

poet, painter, and
printmaker,
William Blake

playwright, poet, and actor,
William Shakespeare

The Bible can uplift and inspire those
that read it's stories and study it.

The stories can inspire you to love others, help others, and grow closer to God.

LET THE BIBLE INSPIRE YOU!

THE
BIBLE

The
BIBLE